Careers without College

Radio Announcer

by David Heath

Consultant:

Mark Braun, Ph.D.
Associate Professor and Chair
Department of Communication Studies
Gustavus Adolphus College

CAPSTONE
HIGH/LOW BOOKS
an imprint of Capstone Press
Mankato, Minnesota

CAPS.

Capstone High/Low Books are published by Capstone Press
818 North Willow Street • Mankato, Minnesota 56001
http://www.capstone-press.com

Library of Congress Cataloging-in-Publication Data
Heath, David, 1948–
 Radio announcer/by David Heath.
 p. cm.—(Careers without college)
 Includes bibliographical references and index.
 Summary: Outlines the educational requirements, duties, salary, employment
outlook, and possible future positions for radio announcers.
 ISBN 0-7368-0172-3
 1. Radio announcing—Vocational guidance—Juvenile literature.
[1. Radio announcing—Vocational guidance 2. Vocational guidance.] I. Title.
II. Series: Careers without college (Mankato, Minn.)
PN1991.8.A6H39 1999
791.44'028'023—dc21   98-46137
                                                              CIP
                                                               AC

Editorial Credits
Karen L. Daas, editor; Steve Christensen, cover designer;
 Kimberly Danger and Sheri Gosewisch, photo researchers

Photo Credits
David F. Clobes, 9, 14, 18, 37
Gary W. Sargent, 12, 45
Jim West/Impact Visuals, 38
Leslie O'Shaughnessy, 6, 22, 30
Mary E. Messenger, 16
PhotoBank, Inc., 4
Photophile, 24
Steve Healey, 27
Unicorn Stock Photos/Batt Johnson, cover; Terry Barner, 10; Robert Ginn, 20;
 Jim Shippee, 32; Jeff Greenberg, 34
Uniphoto/Bob Daemmrich, 29
Visuals Unlimited/Mark E. Gibson, 41

Table of Contents

Fast Facts

Career Title_____Radio announcer

Minimum Educational_____U.S.: high school diploma
Requirement   Canada: high school diploma

Certification Requirement_____U.S.: none
                                                        Canada: none

Salary Range_____U.S.: $7,100 to $102,676
(U.S. Bureau of Labor Statistics and
Human Resources Development   Canada: $12,300 to $64,600
Canada, late 1990s figures)   (Canadian dollars)

Job Outlook_____U.S.: poor
(U.S. Bureau of Labor Statistics and
Human Resources Development   Canada: fair to poor
Canada, late 1990s projections)

DOT Cluster_____Professional, technical, and
(Dictionary of Occupational Titles)   managerial occupations

DOT Number_____159.147-010

GOE Number_____01.03.03
(Guide for Occupational Exploration)

NOC_____5231
(National Occupational Classification—Canada)

Chapter 1

Job Responsibilities

Radio announcers work in the entertainment and news businesses. They help broadcast hours of music and entertainment programs. Announcers also provide important information. Many people listen to radio announcers each day.

Radio announcers have a variety of duties. They read copy on the air. This written information may include news and weather reports. Some radio announcers play music. They also may talk about music they play. Radio announcers may do interviews. For example, they may interview local leaders, musical guests, or other interesting people.

Radio announcers read copy on the air.

Radio announcers work for radio stations. Most announcers begin their careers at small radio stations. These stations often are located in small towns and cities. Radio announcers may move to larger stations when they gain experience. These stations usually are in large cities. Positions at large stations are difficult to earn. Many announcers want to work at these stations.

Radio stations usually have one format. This programming style may be news, music, or talk shows. Some stations mix formats. Mixed formats may include a combination of formats.

Radio Announcer Positions

Radio announcers have different titles and duties. Announcers who announce and broadcast music are called disc jockeys. Disc jockeys often know interesting facts about music and musical artists. They sometimes interview singers, musicians, and other people in the music business.

Disc jockeys announce and broadcast music.

Some radio sportscasters give play-by-play reports from baseball games.

Some radio announcers are newscasters. These announcers read the news on the radio. Some newscasters write the news copy they read.

Radio announcers may be reporters. Reporters sometimes interview people at different events and places. Reporters also give live reports from events as they happen. Reporters may report from accident or crime scenes. They may cover press conferences. Sometimes reporters cover special events such as parades.

Some radio announcers are sportscasters. These announcers report about sports. Sportscasters may announce baseball, football, basketball, hockey, or other sports events. They often give play-by-play reports of sports events. They describe action as it happens. Some sportscasters are color commentators. Color commentators present interesting facts about players and their teams.

Radio announcers may be talk show hosts. Talk show hosts interview people. They may give advice. They may talk about news, sports, and many other areas. Talk show hosts also may take calls from callers. Some callers want to ask hosts or guests questions. Other callers want to talk about their own opinions.

Chapter 2

What the Job Is Like

Radio announcers work at radio stations. Radio stations have the equipment necessary to broadcast radio programs. Stations have microphones, compact disc players, tape players, and transmitters. Transmitters send signals through tall radio tower antennas. Signals are electrical pulses. They become sound when radios receive them.

Radio stations can be AM or FM stations. AM and FM are different types of radio signals. AM signals usually are carried farther than FM signals. But FM signals produce a

Radio towers have transmitters that send signals from radio stations to radios.

DuBOIS

much better sound quality. This sound quality is needed for music. FM stations usually play more music than AM stations. AM stations often feature news and talk shows.

Radio announcers work with other people at radio stations. General managers run radio stations. Program directors help choose programs and music. Engineers operate the electronic equipment. They make sure sound is carried from radio stations to people's radios.

Salespeople sell airtime at radio stations. Airtime is the time when stations broadcast. Salespeople sell airtime in 15-second, 30-second, and 60-second amounts. Businesses buy airtime to advertise their products on the radio. Special interest groups also buy airtime. For example, community officials may buy airtime to advertise events or festivals.

Work Environment
Radio announcers work in booths. These small rooms contain microphones, compact disc

Radio announcers work in booths.

players, cassette players, loudspeakers, and control boards. Some booths have computers.

A radio announcer usually sits at a table or desk. A microphone sits on the table or hangs in front of the radio announcer. The announcer speaks into the microphone. The announcer uses the control board to start and stop music. This board has several buttons that control the compact disc and cassette players. The announcer also uses the control board to turn the microphone on and off.

A radio announcer may listen to the booth loudspeakers as music and advertisements are played. But the announcer also wears headphones. The loudspeakers shut off when the announcer's microphone is turned on. The announcer then hears the program through the headphones.

Silence on the radio is called dead air. Radio announcers must avoid dead air. Radio

Radio announcers wear headphones while working in the booth.

stations depend on music, sports, news, or talk to keep listeners interested. Listeners might change stations if a station has dead air.

Hours

Many radio stations broadcast 24 hours each day. They broadcast seven days a week. Radio announcers often work on weekends and holidays.

Many radio announcers do not work daytime hours. Beginning announcers usually work late at night. They also may work weekends. Fewer people listen to the radio late at night and on weekends. Radio announcers may move to a daytime shift when they have more experience.

Experienced radio announcers usually work during the day. More people listen to the radio at this time. Experienced radio announcers generally are more skilled than

Radio announcers know how to use the booth equipment.

new radio announcers. They are more comfortable on the air. Experienced radio announcers also have more specialized talents. They may know how to write news reports and conduct interesting interviews.

Drive time is one of the best shifts for radio announcers. Many people listen to their car radios during drive time. There are two drive times every day. One drive time is in the morning when most people drive to work. The other drive time is in the afternoon when most people drive home from work.

Some radio stations play recorded programs during holidays. This allows their announcers to take time off on holidays. Radio stations also buy programs from other stations and broadcasting companies. They may play these programs on holidays or late at night.

Drive time is one of the best shifts for radio announcers to work.

**Radio announcers talk on the air for several hours
every shift.**

Personal Qualities

Radio announcers must be knowledgeable to
keep their audiences interested and informed.
For example, radio announcers need to be

aware of current events. Newscasters might read newspapers and news magazines. Disc jockeys might read magazines about music and musicians. They also may go to concerts. Sportscasters might read sports magazines and sports sections in newspapers. They also may go to sports events.

Announcers must be dependable. Their programs begin and end at exact times. Announcers need to be at work on time.

Radio announcers should be good speakers. They need to speak clearly for long periods of time. Announcers talk on the air for several hours each shift.

Radio announcers need to be aware of audience expectations. Many people count on announcers to provide correct information. Many people also expect radio announcers to broadcast programs that are not offensive. Most radio announcers try to meet these expectations.

Chapter 3

Training

Most radio announcer jobs do not require formal education or training. Many announcers train on the job.

Education

Most radio announcers have high school diplomas. Many announcers also take classes at broadcasting schools. These schools offer classes to help students improve their announcing skills. Students learn how to speak clearly. They learn how to use radio equipment. They also learn how to use microphones, headphones, compact disc players, and control boards. Students learn how to write copy. Most broadcasting schools have

Students can take several classes to improve their announcing skills.

small radio stations where students can practice their skills.

Becoming an Announcer

Many people begin their radio careers as interns at small stations. Interns perform various jobs at radio stations. They may answer phones or assist announcers. Interns may not get paid for their work. Some people work as interns at large stations. But positions at large stations are difficult to get.

Some interns are broadcasting school students. These interns may work directly with radio announcers. Radio announcers can help students improve their skills.

Radio stations may hire interns as regular employees. Experienced interns are familiar with the station. They know many people who work at the station. Interns who want to become full-time employees take their work seriously.

Radio announcers keep logs of all the music and advertisements they play.

Radio announcers in the United States and Canada do not need to be licensed. But radio stations must have broadcasting licenses. Stations in the United States must have licenses from the Federal Communications Commission (FCC). The FCC oversees all radio and TV stations in the United States. Radio stations in Canada must have broadcasting licenses from the Canadian Radio-television and Telecommunications Commission.

What Students Can Do Now

High school students can participate in several activities to prepare for jobs in radio. Some high schools have radio stations where students can work. Students also can act in school plays. They can participate in debate and speech. Students can take public speaking courses. These activities can help students improve their speaking skills.

Students may be able to work at school radio stations.

Computer classes are helpful for people who want to work as radio announcers. Radio announcers need to be able to use computer logs. These official lists show the music and advertisements a station plays. Many radio stations keep their logs on computers. Basic electronics classes also may be useful. Radio announcers use electronic equipment such as control boards.

Students also can prepare outside of school for a career in radio announcing. Students who want to be radio announcers should listen to the radio. This helps students learn how radio announcers speak. Students can compare the styles of different radio announcers.

Students also can practice their radio announcing skills with a tape recorder. They can record themselves and listen to how they sound. They can compare how they sound to what they hear on the radio.

Students can learn a great deal about announcing by listening to different radio announcers.

Chapter 4

Salary and Job Outlook

Most radio announcers in the United States earn from $7,100 to $102,676 per year (all figures late 1990s). Radio announcers who work in large cities tend to make more money than those who work in small cities and towns. Radio stations in large cities have larger audiences. These stations can charge more money for airtime. They earn more from advertising. Large radio stations can afford to pay more to announcers.

Radio announcers work in small towns and large cities.

The average salary for radio announcers in the United States is $31,251 per year.

Radio announcers in Canada earn from $12,300 to $64,660 per year. The average salary for radio announcers in Canada is $35,500.

Many stations provide benefits for full-time radio announcers. Benefits are services or payments in addition to salary or wages. For example, some stations provide health insurance for full-time radio announcers. Health insurance helps people pay for health care if they become sick or injured. Some radio stations also have retirement plans. These plans help employees save money for retirement.

Job Outlook

The job outlook for radio announcers in the United States and Canada is poor. Many radio stations use computers to create programs.

Most full-time radio announcers receive benefits.

Fewer jobs will be available as more stations begin to use computers.

Some radio stations also purchase programming from other sources. Stations can buy programs from other stations or broadcasting companies. Some stations broadcast network programs. Network programs are broadcast on several stations at the same time. Radio stations that buy programs need fewer announcers.

It may be difficult to find a job as a radio announcer. But some new radio stations are formed each year. People who train to become radio announcers also develop skills. They may use these skills in other jobs and careers. For example, radio announcers may move into careers in TV.

Some programs are broadcast on several stations at the same time.

Chapter 5

Where the Job Can Lead

Successful radio announcers have many opportunities to advance. They can move into better paying jobs as they gain experience. They also can advance into different positions in broadcasting.

Other Radio Jobs

Radio announcers can move into other radio careers. They can become program directors. Program directors decide which programs will go on the air. Radio announcers can become news directors. News directors decide which news stories to broadcast. Experienced announcers can become station

Radio announcers can move into better paying jobs as they gain experience.

39

managers. Station managers are in charge of entire radio stations. They supervise all the other workers at the stations. Radio announcers can work in sales. Salespeople sell airtime to advertisers.

Getting Ahead

Radio announcers often move from one station to another. Radio announcers with more experience tend to move to stations in larger cities. These stations usually pay higher salaries. Large stations also may offer better benefits.

Popular radio announcers usually advance in their career. Announcers may become popular if they have a special talent. They may be able to make audiences laugh. They may ask good questions to make people think. Announcers may be very knowledgeable and give audiences information.

Popular announcers have better ratings. Ratings show how many people listen to certain radio programs. Station managers want to have high ratings. Stations can charge businesses more money for airtime during popular programs.

Popular radio announcers have better ratings.

Related Careers

Radio announcers usually speak well. People who speak well can work in other areas. They can become TV announcers or TV talk show hosts. They also can do voice-overs for TV commercials. Announcers are heard but not seen when they do voice-overs.

Words to Know

broadcast (BRAWD-kast)—to send out programs on radio

copy (KOP-ee)—the written words a radio announcer reads while broadcasting

disc jockey (DISK JOK-ee)—a radio announcer who plays mostly music

drive time (DRIVE TIME)—the time of day when many people are driving to and from work; many people listen to radio programs during drive time.

format (FOR-mat)—the kind of programs a radio station features; music, news, and talk are different kinds of formats.

intern (IN-turn)—a person who learns a job or skill by working with an expert in the field; many radio announcers begin their careers as interns.

log (LOG)—an official list of what a station plays

radio station (RAY-dee-oh STAY-shuhn)—a place that broadcasts radio programs

ratings (RAY-tings)—numbers that tell how many people listen to certain radio programs

signal (SIG-nuhl)—an electrical pulse transmitted for radio communication

transmitter (transs-MIT-ur)—a device that sends out radio signals

To Learn More

Bliss, Edward. *Now the News: The Story of Broadcast Journalism.* New York: Columbia University Press, 1991.

Cosgrove, Holli, ed. *Career Discovery Encyclopedia.* Vol. 5. Chicago: J. G. Ferguson Publishing, 1997.

Weigant, Chris. *Careers as a Disc Jockey.* New York: Rosen Publishing Group, 1998.

Useful Addresses

Broadcast Education Association
1771 North Street NW
Washington, DC 20036

Canadian Association of Broadcasters
P.O. Box 627
Station B
Ottawa, ON K1P 552
Canada

Federal Communications Commission
1919 M Street NW
Washington, DC 20554

National Association of Broadcasters
1771 North Street NW
Washington, DC 20036

Internet Sites

Broadcast Education Association
http://www.beaweb.org

Canada Job Futures
http://www.hrdc-drhc.gc.ca/JobFutures

Canadian Association of Broadcasters
http://www.cab-acr.ca

National Association of Broadcasters
http://www.nab.org

Occupational Outlook Handbook—Radio and Television Announcers and Newscasters
http://www.bls.gov/oco/ocos087.htm

Index